offering my heart

Ivan Nuru

Copyright © 2017 by Ivan Logan

All rights reserved.

ISBN: 1973949970
ISBN-13: 978-1973949978

For the nights my love felt wasted

For the mornings my love was still there for me

The certainty we both need

I may never be able to give you all of me
That person is still evolving
I may never stop longing to be whole for you
If you ever decide that you don't want to wait
If your longing expires or if my love fails to inspire
here's my love in this poem
I have crafted it into a beautiful harmony
It has the essence of eternity
to remind you I'll love you eternally
I put my love in this poem
because it has a forever we may never possess
A piece of me will never leave these words
I know that we will change for better or worse
but what you're reading right now is
stubborn love
unchanging love
unfading love
If you can't commit to me
here's my heart in poem
My trust in verse
I don't know anything but what I'm writing
and I can't change what's already written
Here's my love if you need to see it written

What's keeping me up at night

1. I feel stuck. I feel like I've been putting pieces together to the wrong puzzle or maybe I'm too scared to see the finish product.
2. I'm searching for the change I need. I'm not sure if I'm ready to give up the things that made me and also, broke me.

    I fell in love with both.
3. I lost my comfort in becoming the person I'm meant to be.

    I don't think that person will accept me.
4. I wish my family and friends would see me for who I really am. I don't want to be remembered for someone who doesn't exist.
5. Sections of my heart are still struggling to find its way back together—my mind went searching for them. I'm in pieces, because you couldn't love a piece of me.
6. I'm finally listening to myself and there's silence, there's absence. I wish I didn't have to be so sorry for myself.
7. God. He's reaching for me. He's reminding me. He's teaching me. He's re-sculpting me. He's preparing me.

flesh

i really try to be comfortable with the skin i wear

i really try to look better for the people that stare

me and shame have this secret affair

how do you wear comfort when no one's there

it's not just society but me too

i'm my own nightmare

trying to be perfect is bad for my welfare

but i need to be perfect to stop this urge to compare

i wouldn't call myself insecure

but damn i wish i was a little more secure

i don't really go to the gym

but i want to sweat off this imperfection

to have a better complexion

less likely to face rejection

i was once your only selection

now i feel like an alternative

because you went to someone else

evoking the me that's sensitive

evoking the me that needs attention

but you only think i'm perfect

when i'm releasing your tension

i have feelings

but you only care when i'm giving you a feeling

Ivan Nuru

my body is love
only accepts love
your touch must
have the intention
of making love
don't be afraid
to get lost in me
you'll find love

liberated

my love is soft
tell me if i'm too subtle
what if i pretended to be good
let's say my heart seeks trouble
you speak my name like it's your obligation
you paint my mind with your foundation
my body is a compass drawn to your location
we are two canvases waiting for illustration
sexual freedom is self-care to ourselves
our insides hold knowledge
that you won't always find on bookshelves
you have to love and touch oneself
and others that makes sense to self
stay close to the man or woman
that treats your body like home and not a motel
stay parallel to what feels right and doesn't repel
if love and sex is obscene
i'm happy to rebel

Mother

Always running
I suppose we do have the same features
They tell me I look like you I suppose they see that anger too
I hear stories of how you left dad
You forced it until pretending drove you mad
Almost like me and every guy I ever had
I wonder why'd you cry every time you said I love you
Do you regret not saying it often
What happened to showing up often
Is it because your mother never showed you love
She never held you with embrace
made something so close feel out of place
Your mother never asked how your day went
You kept your feelings bottled up and anger spilled over
You carried your problems day by day
hoping your mother would notice
It became hopeless
The day never came
and here I am carrying our hereditary pain
The anger spilled over into me
Just like me you know this pain
Just like your mother you won't show it

Father

I don't blame you I know how it feels to need escaping
and everyone and everything outside of home
becomes that escape
I know how it feels to suffocate
I know what it's like to seek thrill
but I don't understand why trade your family for a temporary feel
Being a father isn't one call on Sundays
that turns into he may call one day
I still hope you can be a father most days
I don't remember you anymore
I have created my own picture of a man
Somedays I see an angry man
Somedays I see a lonely man
Somedays I don't see a man
My heart has become so bland
When you thought of having a child
did you have a plan or was this never the plan
Did you ever have this in mind
Do you think you can leave someone identical to yourself behind
When I honor your wishes don't call on Sundays
Don't start calling most days
It's hard for me to love you nowadays

Back in your arms

i use to be a lover

now these limbs don't love the same

i once believed you cared for me

now you just don't care the same

i love so deep

i should be ashamed for accepting a love that's cheap

i'm so in love with someone i can't keep

at 12 am i have these love cravings

i search for you around 1

and lose myself around 3

sometimes i search for lust

mistakes could never keep up with me

by the break of dawn

the sun illuminates my body

shame has come looking for me

because of what happened around 3

it's not right *but feels right*

when i'm back in your arms

foreclosure

only love resides here
so you made a vacation out of me
you faked the feel of home
so i'd always come back for that comfort
always extending your stay
when we both knew it was past due
i never had a sense of where i should be
so in your arms it felt so heavenly
i thought that when you held me
you were loving me
but your impatience only touched me
i knew what you wanted
which was not what i needed
though i always wanted to please you
despite every night feeling defeated
despite every morning feeling alone
despite every evening asking myself
where is home

Broken

Only in my head is there an apology

I hear the guilt

I hear the foundation falling apart that we never built

Our relationship never had structure

but that doesn't mean it was okay to leave me for another

I thought it was fine not to have a label

but that left my mind unstable

You left my mind guessing

You left my mind begging

with a need to know

Are you going to stay or go

again

It hurts explaining to my heart why this keeps happening

There's so much damage but I keep managing

Revolving around your indecisiveness

Living in pain while it grows a thickness

Lately from you I've been needing the apology

I need to hear the honesty

I'm hoping for reasons why you wish you never left me

I need to confirm that I'm not crazy

For defending you in prayer

For defending you against my intuition

For defending you despite not having my own protection

Transcendent

You never told me how beautiful my love was
but I know you thought what I did for you every night was divine
how I drank your sin like the most delicious wine
I thought it was real because it felt heavenly
The way you said my name so breathlessly

fallen

i fly through time for you
even when my wings ache
in pain for you
some nights get so lonely
i need you to take me with you
some nights get so lonely
i need to be taken from you
some nights get so lonely
i forget my value
my wings aren't made for you
but they always fly to you
soaked in lust and love for you
have you ever seen someone
burn in rain searching for you
have you ever seen someone
stuck in a crossfire
dying for a desire

Rebirth

I've decided it was love even if it remains wordless

I've decided I'm going to be the one to give you wings

I'm going to give my mistakes the right to fly

I hold faith in my heart so this isn't goodbye

This isn't my fall but rise to the most high

This is the opening to my third eye

To pain I'm no longer turning a blind eye

I'm making friends with her

She holds a good conversation

Pain isn't here to hurt me

She wants me to outgrow my being

The lonely nights hold meaning

The lonely nights are just the dark before the beginning

The lonely nights taught me a second language I never knew

When you left you gave me something new

I was reborn after your love beat me

black and blue

You don't have to tell me it was love

because I already knew

It just died like all things do

like me before and after you

Why I love you

our weakest moments are greater than any love at its best

for that i talk to God about you

and when i do it's the most passionate subject i ever talked about

i hope he gives us his best

the butterflies have made a home inside of me

they love to flutter when i'm around you

i enjoy the feeling too

you raise my consciousness

your energy has a taste of pureness

i'm addicted to the intake

being with you is when i'm truly awake

i see life with you

i see my life with you

you teach me more about my body than any anatomist ever could

you discover parts of my mind psychology has yet to unfold

you make secrets pour out of me i thought would never be told

you have my heart in a stronghold

wrapped with a blindfold

i don't need to see because you make me feel

i trust you despite this feeling being surreal

When someone says, "I love you" —
know that your idea of love
won't always be the same as theirs.

fragility

weak men aim to belittle
becoming less man little by little
never take what they offer and settle
weak men leave with a better opportunity
they fold under scrutiny
and bend by their own insecurity
weak men lack true flexibility
they think their puberty equals maturity
weak men are paradoxes
not misunderstood
or worth being understood
weak men want your fruit only when it's ripe
it doesn't matter if your love fits just right
they aren't worth trusting out of eyesight
or under your moonlight
weak men just won't be your wright
they won't be there midday or midnight
they only come out with an appetite

The Men you've had

Men that are broken

Men that have no devotion

Men that are lost

Men that are afraid of being soft

Men that don't want to be save

Men that thinks their ego makes them brave

Men that are okay with pain infliction

Men that came with restrictions

To the man scared to love me

i touch you without making physical contact
my energy itself is enough to make you climax
my intimacy only gets more intimate
we break but us making is more sentiment
yet you fight when it gets sentimental
you hate when my love tests your mental
the truth to my love makes you fearful
you hate how real it is
you hate how raw i get
it confuses you how natural it is for me to love you
it's even more confusing you feel it too
you keep resisting
but there are missing spaces in you where i keep fitting
you don't like admitting
as if when we're kissing you're not doing enough revealing
you leave your secrets on my lips
you make trips on my tongue
and get scared when it gets fun
you left this journey in me
this is an expedition you planted
you can't abandon it
you won't desert me
you're going to hurt you *hurting me*

Sometimes

I have to isolate myself when people's energy rubs off on me too much. Sometimes I have to remind myself to remain myself. Sometimes I have to be a little braver to walk away from people and situations that I know don't serve purpose in my life. Sometimes I have to be a little stronger to believe there's purpose in my life. Sometimes I do have to tell myself I love me, because people who say they do neglect to show it. Sometimes I do have to be my everything unless I want to settle as someone's nothing. Sometimes I have to remind myself this isn't all for nothing.

Choosing myself

I choose to stay away from people who leave me with
the feeling of being used
I don't want to be the person you can just choose from
I refuse to be the friend only good for advice
I refuse to be the lover that expires after one night
I am not disposable
I was born with God's forgiveness
though it wasn't birthed to forgive you over and over
I was well crafted for months and shouldn't be treated
like I'm only worth one
My worth isn't defined by your standard of beauty
I wish you could've seen my love as beauty
I wish you could've seen my love as real love
I don't care about your weight or who you dated love
I won't try to control you type of love
I still wait for this
I often pray for this
I wish you could've just said
I'm not capable of loving like this

Reminders

1. It's okay to start over. It's okay to need someone and fail to keep that person. It's okay to trust change. It's okay to put faith in your recovery. It's okay to begin again and find your being again.

2. Your failures aren't your legacy. Your failures help create your legacy. Fail your way into love. Fail your way into finding yourself. Fall short to stand tall.

3. Expect nothing. Expect nothing. Expect nothing. Stop giving yourself to disappointment. Stop giving yourself to him or her. These days I can't expect anything from family or friends. These days I'm not certain if I can expect anything from myself. These days I can only expect nothing.

4. Be human and allow yourself to feel humanly things. Nothing's shameful about being depressed. Nothing's shameful about not knowing the cause or how to get rid of it—or how to get rid of the person causing it. Remember it's okay to be happy too. It's time to start giving ourselves to ourselves. I need more time the more I lose it. You're human it's okay to feel like you're losing it.

5. Pray.

Prayer

When I speak your name in prayer
I'm certain this is the purest form of love I can offer
I'm committed to praying for you
even though I'm not sure if I know the person you are
I guess I pray for the person I know you can become
along with me
I'm committed to praying for me
although sometimes I fail to understand that person too
I feel dead often and prayer faithfully reaches for me
God has been telling me life is in your hands
I'm sorry that they have gone numb
from holding on too long and trying to protect what's not there
I collapse into nothingness and try to make a home out of it
You can't build a home off potential
I'm ashamed I fell in love with it
My grandmother taught me you can't pray and doubt
She also taught me not to gaze at dead flowers
hoping they will sprout

Reaching

I'm constantly fighting urges to reach out to you

My fingertips weep for you

They itch for you

I'm the hand that fed you that you never appreciated

but it steady reach out to you

Don't ignore my heart when you see that it has

broke my rib cage to reach out to you

I'm broken but the pieces of me that love you stay intact

I'm certain that its real when we make eye contact

The feelings haven't change since we first met

I keep reaching for the you I still love

I keep reaching for the you I still dream of

Its past 12 but

I stay up waiting, do you ever do that

I stay up waiting, do you remember when we use to do that

Late at night is when I'm most vulnerable

I think that's when you slipped into me

I stay up wondering who keeps you company

I toss and turn wondering have you found a lover like me

Parts of me like to believe that's not likely

I stay up waiting nightly

I wait for that call

I wait for that sign that maybe you still love me after all

Whiskey

some people may call this desperation
months out of my life but i text you
expressing my love with no hesitation
because i know you think of me on your loneliest nights
when you try loving someone new and they can't get it right
or maybe that's my imagination
but i know i was more than decoration
although i look good hanging from your love
did i look as good falling
you don't look as good with someone else
you don't look as good falling for someone else
it's painful to see you fall for someone else
when i thought we would fly
we didn't get a chance to grow
it's painful seeing us die
but in my heart i still have seeds
around my chest i'm growing weeds
loneliness has me in the state of fatigue
i still have my prayer beads
but right now i need whiskey
i'm trying to forget how you left me

a message i never sent

i had to force myself to stop loving you
do you know how that felt
i struggled to move on
i wish you knew how that felt
hopefully one day you learn how to feel
i wish i didn't miss you still

Surrender

I see the fight you put up

with me you can let your guard down

You can hold your fire

We're both burned by the same flame

We're both scorched by the same cause

When we see each other

I know our hearts have the same pause

Why continue to blacken our hearts

when it's drawn to a light not far away

Just trust

That brilliance could be us

Let me ignite the parts in you

that's been concealed

I promise to shed warmth on whatever's revealed

If you just stop fighting my love

I can return trust back to you

I know you want to be revived

With me I know you feel alive

Losing sleep

Do you mind losing sleep with me tonight
Help get things off my mind like how I wish you were mine
and manifest things I've only imagined in my mind

If only I could get it right
The trusting and deciphering if we're really loving
or is it that made up shit to hide what we're covering

I'm never hiding much
depending on your definition of much
I was real to you but our definitions are very much different
Our love has become the difference
I'm not your preference
I still want you and hope for deliverance

I'd rather talk love, your mother, achieving better
Why you could never handle the pressure
but let's just lose sleep together

Moonlight

Tonight I bathe under the moonlight
I hope to cleanse myself from me
Reflection made things out of sight
Our history is something I'll never be able to rewrite
Pain like this is set in stone
Not having someone like you gets me stoned
Maybe in the next life I won't be this lonely
Maybe I'll find love if I stop being so clingy
Maybe I'll find someone if I stop searching so deeply
Maybe if I was more like them someone would need me
I just want someone to need me
I want this moonlight to give renewal to me
Nights like this I scream for better days
Nights like this I become a banshee
Nights like this I trip over love
Excuse me if I get clumsy
Ending up in anyone or anything that's a little cozy
I know what it's like to undress
not prepared for dirty laundry
So I sit here bathing under the moonlight
Please wash away my past
This time I'll get it right
This time I won't lose sight

When i knew i lost myself

I lost me when it was apparent you weren't coming back

I've become addicted to everything

that make missing you feel like a daze

Do you know how it feels to go days

without a love that you consumed everyday

I knew I lost me when I let love abuse me

but it felt okay in a way

Some parts of me may be forever abandoned in your empty heart

I ran to a place of endings hoping for a new start

I painted over myself hoping you could see art

Why can't I be your muse

Why am I someone you just use

My pride was lost when I constantly begged

My spirit broke when you ignored every word I said

I lost me when I searched for answers online

because I was too scared to talk to you

I was too afraid you didn't want to hear from me

Every day without you I felt embarrassed

because I thought maybe I loved too hard

I lost who I was thinking of you just a little too hard

Endings

Feeling you lose interest does something to my pride

I only know how to be me

Would you rather that person hide

You said you want all of me

Soon you will wish that was a lie

Are you pretending with me

Months later will you leave and say I tried

Promises aren't promised

Our sea of forever will soon be dried

Hope exhausted

Emotion thirsty

We impregnated each other with love

shortly having a miscarry

Young love but it's so scary

Weightless but so much to carry

A dead love floats inside of us

No more strength to try just weary

I know you're losing interest

I'm waiting on your I'm sorry

and you're condolences

because you can't keep up with the appearances

of this pretend love

This dying interest

Patience

Get to know someone before you dive with them, because too late you'll realize this is someone you can't swim with. They will not be able to handle the current or maybe you will not—then you are both drowning when *you only had to get to know each other*.

Reminder:

Healing is beautiful, but sometimes
it feels like the breaking all over again.
It will be painful, but knowing you will survive
is what makes it beautiful.

Amnesia

I let you fill me with promises once more
just to leave me once again
The place behind my ribcage is fruitless
I feel even more useless
I don't know if you ate it or if I just let it rotten
Was I ever wanted before I became forgotten
I'm scared to see my face
because I know there's nothing there
A face is a privilege for the people that know their selves
A face is a privilege for those who will be remembered
or those who have an identity that's not dismembered
Do you know how it feels to be outnumbered
Do you know how it feels to give yourself away
without knowing you're taking away from self
You promised that it wasn't just me and myself
Forever sounded so sweet at the time
I fell in love with your warmth during wintertime
When summer came I barely saw you sometimes
and most times I forget that I'm in my prime
I forget how beautiful I am
I forget to look in the mirror and say *goddamn*
but after love I'm not really sure who I am

Loyalty

Loyalty isn't the amount of pain you can take
from someone you love.
Who taught you loyalty is
staying by someone's side who has left yours.
Loyalty doesn't work like that.
Loyalty doesn't test your heart's limit.
Loyalty does come with a limit.

Wine

What do you feel when I'm speaking to you
Are you listening when I'm speaking to you
Do you hear my love
Do you know how I put you first and above
everything
I put you above the God I pray to
I put my flesh and bone into the man I made out of you
I promised you forever but can't seem to get it back out of you
I'm afraid my prayers no longer get answered
because my priority was someone that never answered
I suppose our future faced a decline
and now I reek of wine
It helps me get by most times
When I'm not breaking hearts
Doing the ones I love wrong
because I became your wrong
I wish this was a different song
I wish we sung it together
I wish you could've made walking away look better
This pain is so ugly
To heal it's going to take more than milk and honey
I need better luck
You said you wanted love but really just wanted to fuck

Can we Just be friends?

I'm not strong enough to watch you love someone else
I can't support you standing with another
My smile was meant for us
I don't want to hear stories of smiles not made by us
My eyes will not see a better person for you
My eyes will see a sad excuse for what should be me
How can you ask me to be friends
As if my love wasn't good enough
So now we just hang out on weekends
We both know how that will end
I don't want to be the friend that's more than a friend
or lover that's more like a friend
I don't want to be your friend after the breakup
If you don't love me enough to makeup

Are you that naïve thinking we can return to that place of friends

My cure to heartbreak

The cure to heartbreak is acceptance. You must accept that you can't get back dead emotions and it's also, important to know there's a greater love for you. It's important to love yourself enough to move on. You can't live in the mindset of thinking you won't ever find someone better, because that mindset blocks positive energy that you need to move on. Love yourself, take time for yourself, and don't expect anything to remerge from the past.

we weren't enough

I almost put up my white flag
but our blood is too painted to call truce
I'm tired of folding my heart's truth
We're too dead to plant new roots
Love ages you and I can't taste my youth

I almost surrendered
I got that weak for you
In love you think you're the top contender
You think he's your treasure
You think he won't bury you
but haven't the lies already swallowed you

I almost survived
then your forever's and reality endings collided
You treated me like your joyride
Your sweet trip to someone else
I taught you to set aside your pride
Your love is something I glorified
Leaving me is suicide but I feel dead inside

The old you

If I could bring the old you back
I wouldn't
You're meant to develop into a person
that's not meant for me

If I could bring the old you back
I wouldn't
The old you won't stay
The old you will grow to leave me

Ivan Nuru

How are you feeling after he leaves
If you feel he may never come back
He doesn't deserve another arrival
Men like this make trips
They don't appreciate homes

Naked

Who is the person you're leaving me for
Who was worth abandoning me ashore
I wonder what it's like to face everything I hoped to be
Someone that looks like paradise
A person that'll make you give up me
Who made you sacrifice me
Who made you think it was okay to drop me off
Who did you pick up
Did they have their thumb up
Were they so damn sexy you forgot about us
Were they so breathtaking you had to stop for their air
then you had to go and make that person my heir
Who is this person
This version of who I should be
Do they know you have someone that loves you already
Do they know that everything you know comes from me
I want to meet this person
I wonder what it's like to see the past face the future
Will they still want you once they see you all over my face
You call that love for someone
I wear you
I don't want to be left naked
for someone you only love naked

Ivan Nuru

Drowning

You didn't dive with me

I can't swim

but I thought you were willing to jump into uncertainty

You left me and the waves taste like regret

Soft blues are turning into a violent burgundy

Making excuses for you is hurting me

Making excuses for you is leaving me numb

with a reminder of something salty on my tongue

Are we too broken to let bygones be bygones

Are we too deep in the dark to ever see dawn

Was I ever worthy or just your pawn

Was it that we skipped stages

Did you miss my changes

I broke for you every night

while giving you bits of my light

while giving you bits of my soul and never seeing yours often

I needed to see yours more often

Now all I have is the ocean and your scent

and a mouth full of things I resent

Waves are so close to my ears

I hear its accent

so calming

I didn't know I was drowning

Save me

Come and be my savior

Sometimes you don't know why you need prayer

You just pray and I just want you to stay

I feel numb too often

I don't mean to free my pain

but it comes with no caution

I've fallen and I keep falling

Please don't grow impatient with my stalling

Save me when I stumble and my silence turns into a rumble

Save me when I'm almost close to you

but my knees start to tremble

Can you save me when loving me is no longer simple

and everything I say becomes a riddle

Can you find me when my heart becomes a temple

with hidden doors and untold secrets

Would you leave if I told you the secrets to my secrets

or would you become a hidden door

and believe I'm not worth saving anymore

You may never understand how I'm a living metaphor

but I promise there's rebirth after my cold war

Don't tell me you don't think you can handle me anymore

What keeps me alive is the love we had in-stored

Save me

empty

I'm collapsing over what's left of myself

I should've loved you less

I should've saved more for myself

There's not enough in me to love anyone else

not even myself

One night

Things don't manifest over night
Be patient
I find myself saying every night
I'm learning to stop blaming myself
over faults and misfortunes
because I can't change in one night
The truth is
I can't choose what's going to happen
I can only choose how I will respond
and hopefully life responds back nicely
and hopefully I find myself
but I know not in one night

Dear old me

I hear you in everyone's laugh
They just can't make it as beautiful as yours
I try to smile more often
That doesn't seem to happen
I need you more often
I can't make peace with sunny days
If I'm not sharing that warmth with you
I don't feel like myself
I only felt with you
I will never let go
not until I reach you again
not until I find the person I use to be
I know you're deep in my bones
Hidden in my heart
Shy amongst my rib cage
I won't rush you to return
but I do miss you

The damage

I know I sparked love in you
I know that it's slowly catching it's blaze
I just won't be the person to see it burn
Your next lover will feel my fires
My love will burn the home you try to make to ashes
My love will show you that relationships create the worse wildfires
and lovers like me leave a reminder of what you can never rebuild
After the fire there will be smoke
It will suffocate your next lover
It will smell like me
It will be difficult to get rid of
I'm sorry that my love is my love
I'm sorry that it's heavy
and the damage will make you wish you never left me
I'm sorry that whoever's after me will beg God for your recovery
You told me that you could handle me
You said slip your love right into me
but baby my love burns and will stick around
until it burns you and your next lover
to the ground
Be careful with the type of people you give up
because the ones like me
will have you rebuilding everything from the ground up

Our mistake

I would like to blame it all on you

It would be easier on my pride to say this is your mistake

but *this is our mistake*

We both conceived this lost cause together

It was entertainment until we both just knew better

We silently promised we would both be each other's shelter

but we couldn't even handle bad weather

I like to say this tragedy is all because of you

and I would still have a home if it wasn't for you

but the truth is I didn't know what comfort was without you

We fell apart and became lone wolves

Forgetting that we are a pack

Why didn't you have my back

How was it so easy to walk away like that

See I want to hate you

I want to say this was all you to pretend like

I'm perfect and my love is flawless

but *this was both of us*

We ran into love thoughtless

We both made each other nauseous

I wish we weren't so faultless

I want to blame you but we both aren't spotless

Is it possible to make our mistakes hurt a little or a lot less

no matter how much you miss me or i miss you,
we both are missing people that no longer exist.

Changes

I want to hear your story

The way you got stuck

How you almost gave up

How every blue moon you still think about it

Tell me about the change

Tell me how you feel about it

Are you feeling these days

Have you made it through the haze

Tell me about your ways

The way you move

How you still love

How you still forgive

How you confront

or are you still putting up a front

Please tell me you gave up your old ways

Please tell me you stopped giving the wrong people praise

When you become comfortable come home

because you aren't alone

Despite what you believe or misperceive

Don't give up because you still have things to achieve

I know you want to feel relieved

and to forget your heart and roll up your sleeve

but the changes will get better for you just believe

forgive yourself

If you look at all your wrong and mistakes as a reason
to outgrow the person you were yesterday,
you'll bloom into someone
radiant and divine.

Don't shame who you were outgrow who you were.

Ivan Nuru

warning

leave

but know that my love is unforgettable

and when no one else satisfies you

your decision to leave will make you resentful

not ever getting someone close to me again will be painful

love is beautiful
it has no face nor boundaries
no limit or fixed image
love is contagious
its weightless
surround yourself with it
don't be afraid to marinate in it
be more open to love
you are a being composed of love
there is never not enough room for love
continue to figure out what love feels like to you
the process of learning love isn't always pleasant
but learning what feels right and what doesn't is always valuable
so keep loving

Dear old me

I haven't forgotten you or how you use to love.
I'm making things right for you;
you deserve a better home to return to.

The update

After I finish venting to myself I'll be empty
My first love was petty
The story goes like it was real but so unhealthy
Your love was addictive
Your love had me hooked
Too late I was diagnosed with depression
I was in love so the symptoms got overlooked
My needs were forgotten and I became blind
because I trusted a love that only lived in my mind
Life got so hard that I only lived in my mind
I wish it was young and dumb like the elders say
but it was real is what my heart would say
It felt like mid-twenties wanting it to just stay
but everything gets old and becomes harder to hold
It's starting to feel like late thirties and I'm running out of time
Eager for love hoping the next guy is the right one this time
Feeling so deep in age but still young
Feeling this pain but still numb
Still haven't learned to love
Afraid of someone real asking me *why can't I love*
I can't blame it on anyone but me
Healing is a job for me
You're so liberated and *I don't know why I'm still empty*

lungs

easy love reminds you it isn't always difficult
it's your song with just instrumental
sometimes it's silent and simple
we forget to love in a way that's typical
we forget to let our tough skins feel something gentle
with easy love you don't have to be careful
it doesn't have to be special
it doesn't have to display potential
easy love is a love that's already there
easy love is the family that's there
easy love is the friend that's there
easy love are the lovers that manifest from thin air
it's that single flare
it's that strangers stare
it's what you breathe in and out
easy love is always there

Reminder:

You are not your past and it doesn't matter if no one chooses to see your delicate change. The only thing that matters is how you choose to see yourself and knowing your own truth.

If someone only choose to see a version of you that lives in the past let them stay there as well.

Ivan Nuru

grandmother

my heart may have developed a little rust
but my blood still pumps trust
i'm putting my faith in him
stay close to God
at this age, you're lucky enough to be close to anything
guidance is important
you don't want to be lost and lonely
do the right thing even if you're the only
being the better you will leave a beautiful testimony
being free is a part of that beauty
in life you'll have to make adjustments
you're better off without attachments
trust your lost
you'll be surprised with your findings
undress your heart from fear and reveal the hidings
you don't have to conceal
everything that's in your heart is well meaning
keep self-seeking
keep self-healing
keep consuming things that leaves you full
protect yourself with your own love and you'll never be homeless
thinking that you aren't your own person to come to is senseless
be good to self because in the end dying with love is priceless

soul search

where do you come from?
what type of love is in your blood?
what type of hurt is in your heritage?
what does karma say about you?
what's keeping you captive in the past?
when did you lose yourself?
have you ever thought of letting go?
do you really think you have a hold
of the old days?
of the old him?
do you really think you're wise enough like the old folk?
were you this empty yesterday?
have you forgotten how to love today?
without love are you even living today?

Running with my love

did you erase me from your memory
was i ever worth remembering
my heart is charging you with breaking and entering
my heart is so scared that it can't love without trembling
the state you left me in is worth remembering
well i remember
you robbed me of a love that i was willing to give
why hit and run
how far do you think you'll go
you think people won't recognize my love
you think you can run with my love without anyone knowing
you think my love is easy-going
it doesn't obey or sits on autopilot
my love is the type that starts a riot
everyone will know the thief you are
everyone will see you for who you truly are
i mean look *baby* we got matching scars
we got broken promises traveling on shooting stars
you think you can leave me like i'm erasable
i don't need confirmation to know i'm not forgettable
you can't outrun an unsettled love
i'm not someone you use and easily get rid of

coffee

i know heartbreak intimately

we talk over coffee

discussing everyone who has left me

my heart is blacker

i wish i knew myself better

i don't know myself enough to hold a conversation

they ask *how are you*

i hold my tongue

i don't want that pain in the atmosphere

i thought this was really going to be my year

people would've really thought i had it together

the way i make the truth disappear

the real me is invisible

not invincible

invisible

but this depression is so noticeable

this depression is so original

who hurts like me

who has it all figured out

maybe i should have coffee with that person

but i know better to know that we are all hurting

we are all drinking something bitter

just hoping it gets better

Change of heart

I put learning me on hold to raise you into a lover
that I never got to experience
I never had the experience
but teaching you love felt natural
The vibe was spiritual
I watched you grow from my soil
Every time I see you I see my soul
Every time I see you I lose my self control
My ego has been telling me that you can't let me go
Like you ain't got memories of me stored in you
Like you ain't got pieces of me left in you
but I've been telling my ego that I have to let go
Every person that learned from me won't stay with me
Like the lovers that left me
Like the friends that no longer speak to me
Like the people who share the same blood as me
My love is meant to fill others to fill others
To love like broken but strong mothers
To heal everyone that suffers
and right now that's me
I raised you into a lover and now it's time to raise me
It's time to break soul ties
It's time to fulfill past due goodbyes

How are you

The flowers planted in me were beautiful
The growth was delightful
but I had to accept that they all die
Someone forgot to tell me love doesn't sprout year round
or that he won't love you all four seasons

I pray about the place that keeps the hurt as a guest
I try not to visit but I wonder has it changed
It's becoming frightening how I'll never forget
how you wouldn't commit

I left gardens in you
I wonder are the plants still alive
I wonder do you loathe my love
for leaving so much of myself in your insides
enough for your heart to always recognize

My love is thick
but I'm fine enough to say
I'm okay

Things my mother didn't tell me

1. Being heartless isn't the cure to being alone. You are never empty and loving less won't leave you full.
2. Changing who you are for someone you want isn't what you need. Its unnatural to rush your development to reach someone else's expectations.
3. Your roots may be planted somewhere, but you can bloom elsewhere. You are not subjected to the place you were born. Find your own grounding. Find where you belong.
4. Whatever makes you love; live for it. After survival, you must have something to live for. If not you won't ever survive. In the end love keeps you alive and truly fighting.
5. Watch the stars. Remind yourself that there's so much more out there than what's hurting you. Release and discover yourself. You'll realize you're more like the stars.
6. Never hold anything in and never let it go with malicious attentions.
7. Love yourself it's the root of all love. Everything starts with you. Everything will end with the way you decided to love.
8. If you ever decide to have children love them in ways I couldn't or failed to...
9. *I love you.*

spitting image

we are almost identical
we wear the same gloom
we love each other like we came out the same womb
but we can't stand each other enough to sit in the same room
we are so much alike
that its haunting almost ghostlike
but who's to blame
sometimes i feel that we're meant to be the same
like the universe made us in pairs
granting us with a life that we are both meant to share
though i will never understand it
or know who i'm speaking to
maybe my parents and ex-lovers too
we both come in two
despite us being the same
you may not need me like i need you
i just hope in your heart you find
enough courage
to come back to someone
like me
like you

Ivan Nuru

The Honest Truth

I haven't smiled much these days
I haven't spoken a word
My tongue isn't present but I'm desperate to vent
People say you can always come to me
but they aren't ready for something this unpleasant
They say you have nothing to be sad about
and that's why I keep people out
They don't know you spend your days in despair
Begging someone who is never there to care
Searching the mirror for value
Praying for rescue
Asking for the strength to just get through
this stage of life that's not in favor of you
This is why I don't smile these days
Depression is becoming more than a phase
This journey I'm on seems more like a maze
How is it possible to genuinely smile these days
It weighs
Heartbreak doesn't leave it stays
for an extended weekend
It mixes you with regret leaving you thinned
When new love comes you can't comprehend
I want to tell you my truth but there's no end

Learning to live in the present

I don't know who or what will stick around for me, so I'm going to enjoy everything while it's here. Things will change and people will leave. I'm certain of that, but I'm also certain of the things that are here now. I'm not going to miss out on the things in my present worrying about the future, so I'm enjoying now. I'm prepared for anything, I'm prepared for change, I'm prepared to *live*.

Sprouting

you can try using who i was against me
the person i am now will look at you
and say i knew that person too
but only i have let go of the past

you can try using who i was against me
the person i am now will sit quietly
spitefully you'll realize you have nothing
miserably you're holding the skin i have shed

you can try using who i was against me
the person i am now will laugh
i will acknowledge the growth from myself on your behalf
i am a whole soul but you only choose to see half

you can try using who i was against me
the person i am now will surpass your negativity
the person i am now will continue to sprout
the person i am now will do it beautifully

Recovery

sometimes i won't speak or be around

that doesn't mean i'm distancing myself

it means i'm protecting myself

not from you but from myself

oftentimes i have a lot going on in my head

that has a lot to do with myself and not anyone else

sometimes silence is the only way i know how to keep it together

oftentimes isolation is me regrouping with myself

help from others is most appreciated

but i have to save myself

i have to teach myself to be a savior for self

people who truly care

will understand that alone time is important

because i can't be the person everyone needs

if i'm desperately needing myself

i grow in silence

i have to hear my heart because it's my guidance

i don't have wings but i am my own guardian

my angel is somewhere deep inside me

sometimes i won't speak

i'm trying to find my angel

i'm trying to be my healer

i'm trying to be my own protector

Release

Forgive yourself for the times you doubted yourself. Forgive yourself for the times you went back despite promising yourself it would be the last time. Forgive yourself for every single time you forgot that you're human and mistakes are momentary. Forgive yourself for every heart that got caught up in the process of learning who you are. Forgive the damage you inflicted on yourself through the learning that you aren't perfect. Forgive yourself for thinking that completion is perfection. Forgive yourself for ignoring the truth—your intuition. Forgive yourself for letting people suppress your soul and take away your wholeness. Forgive yourself for accepting that you won't ever be whole or love again. Forgive and accept that you were wrong about yourself. Forgive every mistake, every false move into the wrong heart, every misjudgment about yourself, every neglect upon self, and forgive yourself for ever thinking you aren't worth redemption.

i'm not something you consume all at once
you taste me in pieces
thanks to the people that left me in pieces
i'm sweet if you catch that piece of me
i'm soul food if you reach that god in me
i'm always enough
don't worry about not getting fed with me

Alignment

I abandoned trying to change people.

I desire to change my surroundings.

To be more aware of people's attentions

and how things feel.

I believe the universe put things in place

when your heart and mind is in the right place.

Before you fall in love with me

Before I give you all of me

That person you've been wanting

Are you realistic

I'm tired of being rejected

For not being the lover that was dreamt of

For not being the lover I never promised to be

Understand me

Understand that I'm capable of love

but that doesn't mean I'm a machine

or maybe I am like the ones from back in the day

Long lasting but easily replaced by something new

but believe me I'll always fall through

If you stick with me you'll see my truth

and say those new ones don't come like you

My love is like old r&b

If your love doesn't sound like that you can't sing with me

Do you want all of me

My ups and downs

My blooming and wilting

Are you going to add onto what I'm building

My love may be a little rusty but I still need someone worthy

I need actions and not a mouth that's wordy

and someone that will always remember my love is a courtesy

Visionary

i hate how visionary i am

i see the lover you can be

yet that person doesn't exist

but i see it

so i keep trying

because when i see something

i hurt myself until it's no longer a vision

i have to touch it although it isn't always pleasant

that's the thing about being a visionary

what you see doesn't always result in what is

sometimes you see the person they are

but won't accept what is

so maybe i can't accept who you are

because i believe there's a greater love in you

i envision making a lover out of you

We still have a home

we ruined ourselves so many nights
but the morning gave us just enough to recover with
each other
we may be forever unskilled at this love thing
but that doesn't mean we should ever stop building
our walls collapsed
because we threw endings at each other
but i picked it up to mold a beautiful beginning
i swept away the dust with hands full of hope
i lit incenses to let love know our home is still inviting
i opened our stubborn doors to let the old us back in
i believe we can fix this broken place
in agreement the birds are singing
our bed yearns for our weight come lay with me
our home is waiting for us to pay our dues to commitment
stay with me
let's rebuild and redeem
love and everything else in between
let's be dumb teens but by all means
i'm determined
to open these curtains and let light fill us
we can't stop here pretending like we don't have a home
it may need some work but we still have a home

The victim

How many times has he hurt you
If he's pretending like he's the one wounded
If he's pretending like he's the one bruised
He doesn't care about you healing
or how you spend nights weeping
How many times will you let him play you
How many times will you let him play the victim

The games we play

I still got anxiety from a time I did the wrong thing

I still ask for forgiveness for worshiping

A lover who only stays in the spring

I'm still waiting on the love you promised to bring

The joy and antidote

from a time I swallowed a love note

that promised me something sweet

but only gave me a quickened heartbeat

Have you forgotten our past that's incomplete

Are you scared of being complete

Scared of touching wholeness with me

Close to my heart I hold that time we were exclusive

Why are you bent on making our memories illusive

Why do you need to forget us this bad

Before war I thought they said never leave behind a comrade

No matter how bad

I still have no regrets

Even despite that night we played Russian Roulette

I know you're still suffering and recovering

Why are my apologies pending

Why do you only need me depending

Why you act like you got shot playing Russian Roulette

Acting like you're the one that nearly died for us is disrespect

12 am astrology lessons

study my body like constellation

watch my lips move

digest my every word

in conversation

let me be your astrology

be soft and let my love give you an apology

that life has failed to

don't speak i can make your body talk audibly

don't leave i know you feel the nights generosity

gravity

We traveled to the moon just to defy gravity
We saw how much of our love resembles the galaxy
There's something so deep we can't see
There's tons on the surface we don't understand
As long as there's love we'll never fall and continue to stand

We traveled to the moon just to find ourselves
I met a star that resembled your love
ablaze and beautiful
Burning away my flesh and giving me new skin to love
I never felt more on fire
You gave my flames the light to aspire

We traveled to the moon just to give it new phases
Giving it full endings and new beginnings
Our love is always in the state of crescent
Share with me this adolescent
Feel what's present
Love is our present
Our love is beyond humanity
We traveled to the moon and defied gravity

I'll be patient

The universe brings us back together just to take us apart
and every time I play my part and love you
like I've never been taken apart
You know my heart
You know how I wait for you to come back
You know how I ignore the signs given by my zodiac
At this point I have enough hurt to count my scars
At this point I sit counting the stars
For you I've learned to be patient
Without you I'm just vacant
Saying I love you is just an understatement
Did I tell you how I've grown patient
I really wait for forever
I really can handle the pressure
Before the universe take us apart
put me back together
Tell me I'm not stupid for waiting on forever

It takes losing what you think is love to find love
　It takes being fluid to keep something solid

Promises to be there

I don't want to be your wings
I want to fall with you
I don't want to be your light
I'd rather share the darkness with you
You don't need a method of healing
I promise to God I'll die with you
Till death do us part
I'll never break my vows with you
I'm your equivalent
I'm your love that's everything
but innocent
Here's my blessing in exchange
for your consent
for lifetimes
of unconditional love and sex
Do you feel my love in this moment
Don't question what's next
I know every day gets harder
So tell me when you need to be loved harder

Pride

To love means to understand. Love and understanding are practiced in unison. When you take away understanding you seed hate into love. Love shouldn't be divided. Love is simply love and that is something many do not understand. Since there is lack of conscious; lack of love follows. To accept a lifestyle is not the equivalent to living that lifestyle. It's such a shame that people resist to understand someone's way of love. There should not be a war, but many people are fighting for the right to love.

Ultimately,

love always wins.

Recipe

a dash of greed
a grain of the type of women he loves
a pinch of who you use to be
a sprinkle of the pride you have left
the aroma fills the house
it makes you sick to your stomach
the person you've ripened into
barely alive without the love that gave you life
you sharpen the knife
and cut your heart into small pieces
using only the parts that hasn't been used and bruised
or heavily mistake infused
you tell him i hope you picked up an appetite
meaning i hope you haven't been picking up anyone else
he takes one bite and says damn
he loves the thickness of your jam
then there's your subconscious saying
once he's hungry again he will not have a taste for you
and you watch as he devours the last pieces of you
wishing you would've added a cup of regret

To those who are wondering

If you have to guess what someone is feeling for you,
that means they aren't feeling enough or anything for you.

Ivan Nuru

What you should say to him

I gave you a toxic amount of right over me

that made you think you were essential

I gave you so much undeserving praise

that made you think I'd stay due to potential

I fed your ego every night

making you believe you were special

Godlike and irreplaceable

Breathing down my neck irresistible

Filling me with lust that love was no longer visible

Making my nerves dance and do the unthinkable

but now you're so predictable and a life with us is mythical

Your body is a fantasy

but I need more than vanity

I need better than lies and casualties

I'm sorry I'm not staying another night

pretending like this feels right

pretending like this isn't killing me

Leaving me with more trauma

Further away from nirvana

More distant from self

Watch me from a distance and see I'm better off with myself

You're not needed or wanted

I'm going to leave you and leave you haunted

grief

he comes back to you once he has lost it all
this is not love
this is his grief

you fit into his wounds
you comfort his wounds
but once he heals
your love won't compliment the man you have restored
this is when his grief is over

Like you

i want to live like you
free to leave with no regrets
able to bury without paying respects
prepared to disappear when things get complex
i want to live like you
making it look so perfect

i want to live like you
able to live without someone like me
able to live as someone like you
making numbness look so full of life
i want to live like you just living life
being a beautiful conflict
making it look so perfect

i want to live like you
without mistakes
doesn't know the meaning of heartbreak
doesn't know the meaning of longing or to ache
you seem like you got it all correct
making it look so perfect

Love's Prisoner

you asked me was i staying
as if i really have a choice
i always forget to listen to my hearts voice
i always forget to stop drinking the sour milk you spill
that tastes like neglect and us going downhill
they say just run but i only have the will
to stay

you asked me am i staying
because you know how toxic you are
this time you gave me a warning
but this time i felt immune
or maybe numb
i stay believing there will be a different outcome
or possibly freedom

Behind closed doors

It's your voice that make lies worthwhile

When you say you know I'm yours

Gets my lips hostile

It's how you lie in different styles

You fuck me up with your smile

then I'm in your bed of denial

You know I'm yours

You know I'm yours

You know I'm yours

I'm yours I respond knowing this will leave sores

What happens behind closed doors

stays behind closed doors

because I'm only yours

only behind closed doors

Last night

I know fear so well

but you could never tell

Were you destroying or rebuilding me

I could never tell

Kiss me and make my fears go away

Kiss me and don't tell

Maybe you're the one slipping fears in me

I could never tell

Love is so feminine

but you only know how to be male

You don't know how to stay

You only know how to set sail

I put my love for sell and without me you took sail

but I know you so well

You're coming back

Maybe we're killing each other

but we're always coming back

I'm so scared and

love is so scarce

Loving you is the only thing I know

but that's why I'm so scared

and love is so scarce

We're wasting it when love is so scarce

Ivan Nuru

Euphony

your poems are so irresistible
you treat the heart with such tender
love effortlessly surrenders
your poetry makes my mouth water
almost having an orgasm on its own
your poetry makes my inner celestial being moan
i want more while losing sight
stuck seeing the truth and what use to be
there's something so twisted haunting me
how your poems are no longer about me

Keep digging

I thought if I repeated we're done like a mantra

it'll be true but I'm still not over you

Please come home

Meet me at the safe house

Meet me at the graveyard love was buried

Let's dig because our love couldn't have died

Please don't be terrified

I just want this emptiness to subside

I'm not losing it

Keep digging for our love before we lose it

I know I said I was done

but sometimes I'm a hypocrite

I know this will add to my shame

I can hear my mother's wit

Hey, my name is Forgotten

I'm an addict and my love is erratic

I'm not too shame to say that I need you

You're the only one that can handle me when I'm dramatic

I know our love is still alive and that's why I'm at this graveyard

I've survived drowning without a lifeguard

God accepted me every time I died for you on the churchyard

So, I know we aren't impossible

Keep digging for the old us because this is just an obstacle

Ivan Nuru

Lost every friend

We were different people back then

So young

We didn't know who we would become

We made mistakes and had fun

We stayed out getting lost under the midnight sun

Then we lost each other

because we lost ourselves

It's nothing too personal

but the people who we use to be is far from replaceable

 I wish I could place us back together and make things stable

but we experienced this thing called growing

and growth isn't growth without the hurting

I lost my friends because things end

I feel that I had to fall alone to transcend

I lost my friends because this is life

This is losing and failing to keep

This is crying over endings and losing sleep

I wish I still had them for the nights I still weep

I lost my friends because

there's always a means to an end

but the truth is I really don't understand

I just pray the future holds a greater plan

Metamorphosis

You're nothing close to him

but you're decent so I settled for someone like you

I'm sorry I see you as his residue

The last flower so I suppose you'll do

Then my heart started wanting you

Then you started to become more like him

Less

You started to change

as if me starting to care was strange

How can you detach from me

when you're the man that I nourished

Why do I feel dead the more you flourish

Why did you become just like him

My subconscious responded *because you wanted someone like him*

Dying passion

when you put your head between his inner thighs

you gave him passion

but he left and gave people something to gossip about

i promise they'd hold their tongues too

if they tasted abandonment

after pouring out everything in them passionate

they'd fall on the battlefield if their wings were gun down

they'd feel suck too if a man pinned their heart down

they'd feel empty too if a man took everything he found

you watched your world fall in front of you like

the night you begged at his feet to stay

now the world looks at you with regret

the same eyes he gave you

you can't change because you gave him

something permanent

something passionate

now you're sick every night because he treats someone else right

how someone else is flourishing life

along the roads you created for him

you spoke so highly of him but you're six feet under

stuck trying to surrender

wondering how could one man give you so much to remember

Remember

he's already shown you the truth

there's no need to justify it

he's already made his exit

some nights will get desperate

some nights will be unpleasant

but don't be his cesspit

don't wait for him to return

don't look at the person he's loving waiting for a turn

it's going to be hard to unlearn

it's going to be hard to not feel scorn

but it's okay to take time to mourn

to feel sadness

to feel like you're not feeling anything

after being numb for so long

going back feels like the right thing

but remember

to him you're just another number

you're just pleasure

nice lips and being sexier than ever

won't hold you two together

making excuses time after time

won't bring you forever

remember

presence

he's not the best you have in life
he's not the best you have now
you are the best you have now
you can treat yourself better than he does
you don't need him to remind yourself that

you are loved
you are loved
you are loved

Trying to hold on

It's out of my hands but if I had more

I would force you to make healthier decisions

If my hands held enough love

I would mold your heart into a better condition

If only my hands held a religion

that would make you believe in yourself

I could hold you

I could whisper I love you more than myself

It could be so heartfelt

so overwhelming

almost compelling

but it will never be enough to make you love me

Most importantly it's not enough to make you love yourself

I see you self-destructing

I see you falling

My hands aren't enough to rebuild bridges

or catch all your misses

Numbness may taste delicious

but it isn't healthy

It isn't wholesome

My hands are too full to write your poem

If you don't change you will be lonesome

and I will be long gone

Ivan Nuru

Conversations with Luna

You were my inspiration to love

I'm feeling more deprived

than most of my emptiest nights

I long for the moon to tell me where you are right now

Who and how are you choosing to love right now

I asked the moon *could she teach me how to be beautiful*

surrounded by darkness

I asked her *do you know why he was so heartless*

From my losses I've built a fortress

I live in pain

The moon finally responded

She asked *how could I live this way*

how could you lose your way

I wept

I said *I lost him and more of my self-respect*

The moon said *reflect*

you have a heart to protect

the more you damage it the more you lose your flow

She said *I'm alone yet I constantly glow*

You leaving influenced me to forget love and give up

Then the moon taught me how to recover

Then the moon said **no** *only you're capable of truly lifting yourself up*

because you may have me now but not when the sun comes up

Origin

Change is not a concept
Change is a woman
I belong to change
I belong to her
A sacred body of literature
Women are needed
Women are stitched with passion
Delicately seeded
Women embody change
We must treat them better
Women are treasure
Let's start being more like the woman
Let's start with changing

waiting

Were you busy tonight

Did you turn into a train

Was your destination someone else

I bought a ticket

The 9:00 pm one

I waited for you

Maybe I missed you

or maybe you were off to someone else

Did you forget that I'm your 9:00 pm

Did you forget that I built you

I laid down the foundation

How can you give someone else rides on my creation

I gave you freedom and flexibility

but not to test how far my patience can stretch

I waited and waited and waited for you

then here comes the 9:00 pm

You didn't stop but I saw that someone else

It was enough to see that I didn't matter anymore

but I know you will still see me much more

I laid down the foundation and taught you love

You will see my heart on every passenger

at every station

Next time don't forget to stop at your 9:00 pm location

I miss you

The walk down this street feels like you
Feet against pavement feels like your heart
Tough yet pierced through temptation
Never ending series of roads
Love hits me like an intoxicated driver
Sometimes I'm the drunk
Walking seduces me
because I feel closer to you every step
Never ending series of roads
More traffic
but I still see you
Red lights become tempting
I see you
Chasing you is worth it
because I must reach you and fill in this pit
It's not you I'm running to
It's me

Wanderer

My apologies
if you thought I was committed to your lies
I committed to what I thought was love
We ended but the search for it won't ever stop
even when I'm lonely and I feel like coming to a stop
My heart is still looking for a place of belonging
even when it gets heavy from longing
It was nice of you to keep this emptiness at bay
but we both know neither of us are meant to stay
It would be nice to look at endings and disobey
Some nights I still wish we made it all the way
It would've been nice
but constant regret isn't paradise
Each time I forgave you was like déjà vu
You told me I wouldn't smile without you
but leaving was my great rescue
Life is my adventure
I'm it's wanderer
I'm it's secret lover
I didn't find happiness with you
but that doesn't mean I won't ever find it without you
Finding love is an adventure and
you can't stop a wanderer

Pack

i wept all night

it turned into a howl

the wolves heard me

my pain had them running to me

they became my one true family

they're listeners

they heard my whispers

and felt my cries

i have a thirst for freedom

an instinct for loyalty

i used to cry

now i howl

i run with the wild

Last apology

I am sorry that I wasn't the person from your dreams
I am sorry that my love wasn't beautiful enough to wake up to
I am sorry that I could not wake up love in you
I am sorry that I wasn't funny enough
but the way I gave myself to you will make nice jokes
but I am sorry I didn't see the joke in you giving me
a sweet heartbreak
I am sorry that I don't want to be your sweet mistake
I am sorry that I wasn't a slave to your needs
I am sorry that I wasn't your one night stand without needs
I am sorry that I care about your wellbeing
in a way that makes you insecure
I am sorry that my belief in you
is something you can't seem to find in yourself
I am sorry that I'm finding it easier to move on and love myself
I am sorry that you will remember me in everyone
I wish too that my love showed more modesty
I am sorry that this is the last apology

for the ones scared to be loved

It's addictive to love someone that doesn't love you back,
because you're not fearing them actually loving you back.
Stop giving yourself to people who won't ever love you.
Love the ones who love you and face your fear of being loved.
You deserve to be loved.
You're so worthy of it.

Whenever you're ready

Sometimes the problem isn't opening up to someone else—
the problem is opening up to yourself.

You have to be ready first.

You have to have an open relationship with yourself first.

and it's okay to not be ready, but when you are..

Allow your love to be unafraid.

Allow your love to love and be loved,

but only when you're ready.

To the next person I love

I hope you stay for what's real
I hope you welcome everything I reveal
After honeymoon phases I will love you still
After some time I pray we keep the thrill
I'm not ideal
I'm not what you get from the movies
I've heard behind the scenes are ugly
I don't want to say you're lucky
more like blessed to have me
I'm an open book ready for your ink
Pierce my mind with the things you think
Always tell me what you feel
Let our connection be more than sex appeal
When I fall deeper in love with you
whisper to me that its real
I'm ready to do the imaginary
I'm ready to bring you flowers in February
I'm ready to be that someone you want to marry
I'm ready to give you a love that's healthy and sweet
I'm ready to stop your search and heartbeat
just to fill in the missing ones

because I'm the one

love me how i love you

believe in me
when i can't believe in myself
tell me i need the same love i give to you
can you love me enough to say
keep some for yourself
drink as much love as you spill
can you come aboard when i'm about to wreck
can you bring peace to my deck
do you possess a certainty
because i don't want to wonder anymore
but if i trail off can you meet me at the end
can you promise me if we have one it'll be a beautiful end
promise that you see me for who i am
and you're not hoping for a great change
but that you see one with us
i'll never change on us
but can you remind me to not change on me
remind me that love is still in me
i'll never forget how to love you
but sometimes i forget how to love me

Healing

I got mentally sick believing that you were the one meant to take care of me. After falling in love with you and not receiving much love back—I realized making sure I'm okay is a job for me. loving myself is my top priority. No matter who lacks love for me will not matter as long as I'm loving me.

The trooper you didn't deserve

I'm not sure what feels right anymore

but I do know what feels wrong

I forgot how to be strong

Like being alone after abandonment

Like rejection after rejection

Like putting your heart on the line without protection

Like I wish I had that complexion

that makes people think you're fine

I forgot how to be strong

once I realized you were never mine

What was I thinking during that time

Sections of my heart wasted

I can't think of you without being intoxicated

I've learned how to gracefully smile to people

with teeth full of hatred

I got badges on my chest

for being loyal with the most bruises

I got badges on my chest

for a heart that still loves with the most uses

I'm not sure what these badges will get me

but I know what I've done for you

and I know you know too

In my past relationships

I've been kissed by many souls, but very few touched my soul. I don't know what it's like to be lit on fire by passion; only lust. Every lip placed on me smelled of hunger and not appreciation. A sweet tooth they all had, but a sweet heart not so much. So, when I'm asked about love I always mistake it for lust. Love and lust both share four letters, but one gives you a feeling that lasts for a moment and the other... *well ask someone whose been loved.*

fearless

Every single time I lost myself in people or things;
I gained a piece of me that knows how to love
myself better than the person I lost.
I'm not afraid of losing myself,
because I know I will always find someone better.

Planting Security

Insecurity damages what's meant for you.
There are glorious things promised to you
and even more honorable things you're deserving of.
Don't let insecurity take what's meant for you away.
You don't have to be insecure about anything,
because someone like you is capable of everything.

about Ivan

Ivan Logan, known as "Ivan Nuru", is a writer based in Mississippi. Ivan's work is inspired by experiences and the art of healing. He spends most of his time reading and writing poetry. He welcomes everyone in need of love and hope, and that is when the poetry is found.

For more from Ivan Nuru keep up with him on social media

Twitter/Instagram: @IvanNuru

Made in the USA
Lexington, KY
02 April 2018